DATE DUE

0

GAYLORD   PRINTED IN U.S.A.

KELP FORESTS

By Melissa Cole

Photographs By Brandon Cole

BLACKBIRCH®
PRESS

THOMSON
GALE

JACKSON COUNTY LIBRARY SERVICES
MEDFORD, OREGON 97501

San Diego • D   Maine • London • Munich

Photo Credits: Cover, all photos © Brandon D. Cole; illustrations by Chris Jouan Illustration

LIBRARY OF CONGRESS CATALOGING-IN-PUBLICATION DATA

Cole, Melissa
  Kelp forests / by Melissa Cole.
    p. cm. — (Wild marine habitats)
Summary: Discusses what kelp forests are, what makes them unique, where they are found, what plants and animals make up their food webs, and what impact humans have on these fragile ecosystems.
Includes bibliographical references and index.
  ISBN 1-56711-909-3 (hardback : alk. paper)
  1. Kelp bed ecology—Juvenile literature. 2. Kelps—Juvenile literature. [1. Kelp bed ecology. 2. Kelps. 3. Marine animals. 4. Marine plants. 5. Ecology.] I. Title II. Series: Cole, Melissa S. Wild marine habitats.

  QH541.5.K4C65 2004
  577.7'8—dc21   2003010091

Printed in the United States
10 9 8 7 6 5 4 3 2 1

Contents

Introduction

There are many different types of habitats in the world's oceans. A habitat is a place where certain animals and plants live together naturally. One specific ocean habitat is a kelp forest. Kelp is a type of brown seaweed that grows up from the ocean's floor. Groups of these plants form a kelp forest, which is a thick, junglelike, underwater habitat.

Groups of kelp, a brown seaweed that grows from the ocean floor, form kelp forests.

Kelp forests are often found within a few miles of the shore. They grow at depths of 120 feet (36.5 m) or less. Kelp grows best in nutrient-rich waters where temperatures stay below 72°F (20°C). Kelp forests are common off the Pacific coast of North America from Alaska to Mexico's Baja peninsula. They are also found along the coast of South America near Chile and Peru. In the Atlantic Ocean, kelp forests grow near Argentina and off the tip of South Africa. Kelp surrounds many islands in the Antarctic Ocean. It also thrives in the Tasman Sea, off the coasts of southern Australia, New Zealand, and Tasmania.

Kelp forests usually grow in nutrient-rich waters within a few miles of the shore.

5

What Makes Kelp Forests Unique?

Kelp forests are unique because they are made up of the largest, fastest-growing plants in the sea. Other plants found in the ocean are much smaller than kelp. Giant kelp can reach lengths of more than 150 feet (46 m) and grow more than 2 feet (60 cm) in a single day! Since kelp plants are so big, they provide shelter for many animals that would otherwise be forced to live on a bare, rocky reef.

Kelp is the fastest-growing plant in the ocean and can grow more than two feet in a day.

Climate

Kelp forests are greatly affected by seasonal changes in the weather. In the summer, when the seas are calm and there is plenty of sunlight, kelp forests grow to be thick and healthy. Winter brings strong winds, fast currents, and huge waves. These forces can tear the kelp plants and rip them from the ocean floor. The forest then becomes much thinner. There is less cover for the creatures that live there. The lower parts of the kelp, the rootlike anchors called holdfasts, usually survive, though. In the spring and summer, these plants regrow and form a new kelp forest.

Holdfasts are the lower parts of the kelp that help anchor the plants to the ocean floor.

The kelp forest is made up of three main layers. Specific types of plants grow within each layer. The top layer of the kelp forest is called the canopy. Giant kelp is the most common species in the canopy. This kelp grows up from the bottom of the forest and spreads out along the water's surface. It forms a mat of leaves and stems, called blades and fronds. This mat creates shade for everything below it.

The top of the kelp forest, or the canopy, provides shade for the plants below.

The second layer of the kelp forest is known as the understory. In this middle layer, smaller species such as winged kelp, bull kelp, and oarweed fill the spaces between the giant kelp stalks.

The understory is the middle layer of the kelp forest, where various species of kelp grow.

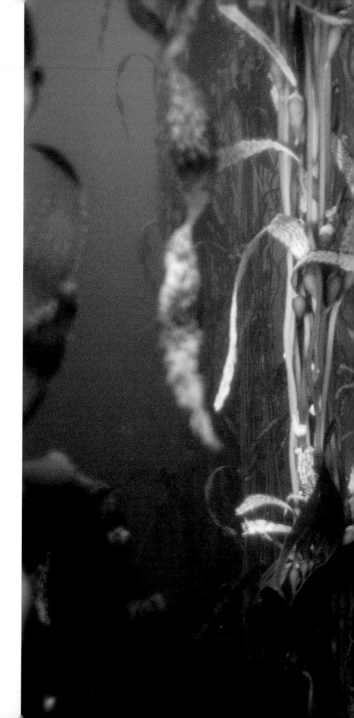

The third layer of the kelp forest habitat is the kelp forest floor. This layer is found on the rocky reef beneath the understory and canopy. Plants such as rockweed, red algae, and coralline algae live in this layer. They grow in between the kelp holdfasts. These smaller plants provide important hiding places for many animals, such as crabs, fish, and shrimp, which live on the forest floor.

Kelp plants have many adaptations that allow them to survive in this habitat. Holdfasts release a gluelike substance that cements them to the rocky reef. This strong grip on the reef keeps the kelp plants from drifting away during storms.

Crabs, shrimp, and fish hide among the small plants that grow on the kelp forest floor.

Another adaptation that helps a kelp plant survive stormy weather is the flexible stem, or frond. Fronds help kelp plants withstand all but the strongest currents and waves, because they bend rather than crack into pieces. These stems are not stiff enough to hold the kelp plants upright, though. Instead, a kelp plant has small bladders, or gas-filled bulbs, at the base of each blade, or leaf. Together, these bladders act like balloons and lift the whole plant up toward the surface.

Hundreds of species of animals live in and visit the kelp forest. Specific types of animals prefer each different layer of the kelp forest. For example, many animals take advantage of the kelp forest canopy. Harbor seals rest in the canopy during the day. Then they feed on squid and fish in deep water at night. Along the North American coast, sea otters spend much of their time floating in the kelp forest canopy. Sometimes they dive down to the reef below and feed on urchins, crabs, abalone, and octopus. At night, otters roll around in the canopy to wrap themselves in the kelp. This keeps them from drifting away while they sleep.

Many types of fish hide among the kelp plants in the understory layer. Many of these fish can camouflage themselves, or blend in with their surroundings. Schools of silvery blue rockfish swim in and out of the kelp plants and blend in with the water. Giant kelp fish hover between the kelp fronds. These fish are slender and golden brown, so they look like kelp. Camouflage allows kelp fish to hide from enemies such as harbor seals and hunt smaller fish and shrimp without being seen.

Sea otters (opposite) and harbor seals (right) relax in the forest canopy and dive underwater to feed.

In the kelp forests of South Australia and Tasmania, a fish called a leafy sea dragon also uses camouflage. This rare cousin of the sea horse matches the color of kelp and has leafy growths all over its body. It looks just like a piece of floating kelp.

Larger animals also visit the kelp forest understory in search of food and shelter. Sea lions feed on fish and crabs. They find prey with their sensitive whiskers and excellent vision. Sleek sharks prowl the borders of the kelp forest. They are attracted by the large schools of silvery fish as well as the seals and sea lions.

The leafy sea dragon looks just like a piece of floating kelp.

A different group of animals lives on the rocky reef below the understory. The kelp forest floor is carpeted with colorful animals such as starfish, anemones, and sponges. Anemones often attach themselves to kelp holdfasts. They feed on tiny floating plants and animals called plankton. On the kelp forest floor, abalone and sea urchins crawl along in search of loose kelp blades and algae to eat.

Starfish, anemones, abalone, sponges and nudibranchs (inset) live on the kelp forest floor.

15

Many animals have adapted to life on the kelp forest floor by blending in with their surroundings to hide from predators. Creatures such as crabs, fish, and octopuses hide in caves and crevices along the reef. Masking crabs cover their bodies with bits of kelp and sponge to disguise themselves. These crabs look like part of the reef.

Bottom-dwelling fish benefit in different ways from their coloration. Camouflaged fish such as red Irish lords, kelp poachers, and warbonnets hide within clumps of algae, soft corals, and sponges. Other fish, such as the garibaldi, are brightly colored and do not blend in with their surroundings. In nature, such bright coloration sometimes warns predators that an animal is either poisonous or dangerous. Garibaldis fiercely defend a territory that often includes a shelter hole, feeding area, and breeding site.

The bright coloration of some bottom-dwelling creatures warns predators that they are poisonous or dangerous.

Other fish that may be found along the kelp forest floor are predators. Large fish such as lingcod, cabezon, and black seabass rest near the bottom. They are quick to gulp down unwary fish that swim by. Wolf eels live in caves and crevices in the rock. These long, flabby-skinned animals have powerful teeth and jaws. They can crunch through spiny sea urchins, crabs, and scallops. The Pacific giant octopus lives in the kelp forests of the Pacific Northwest. This animal is the world's largest octopus. It sometimes grows to more than 20 feet (6 m) from arm tip to arm tip. The Pacific giant octopus usually hides in caves during the day. It hunts for crabs, clams, and fish at night.

Scavengers such as starfish, shrimp, worms, and lobsters, which also live along the bottom, are very important to the kelp forest ecosystem. These animals feed on natural waste, such as drift kelp and dead animals that sink to the bottom. This keeps the kelp forest floor clean.

Wolf eels (top) and large fish such as the cabezon (middle) and lingcod (bottom) are powerful predators that live on the forest floor.

Food Chain

All creatures need to feed or gain energy to live. In a kelp forest, energy in the form of sunlight is used by kelp to make energy. When a kelp crab eats the kelp, some of the plant's energy becomes part of the crab. When the crab is eaten by a seal, which in turn is eaten by a shark, the energy is passed from creature to creature. When the shark dies and sinks to the bottom, scavengers such as starfish and lobsters feed on the remains. Decomposers such as worms, sea cucumbers, and bacteria break down the last bits. Any leftovers mix with the water. Kelp absorbs these nutrients through pores in its fronds and blades in addition to the energy that it receives from the sun. Then the whole cycle begins again.

This process of energy passing between organisms is called a food chain. Several food chains linked together are called a food web. Ecologists use food web diagrams to show the relationship between organisms living together in a habitat community.

In the kelp forest food chain, worms (inset) and other decomposers are just as important as large predators.

A Kelp Forest's Food Chain

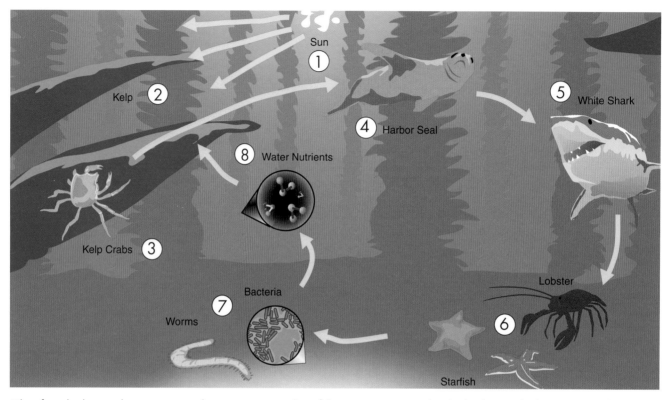

The food chain shows a step-by-step example of how energy in the kelp forest habitat is exchanged through food: (1) Sunlight is used by (2) kelp to make sugar. When a (3) kelp crab eats the kelp, some of the plant's energy becomes part of the crab. When a (4) harbor seal eats the crab, and then a (5) white shark eats the harbor seal, energy is passed from creature to creature. When the shark dies, scavengers such as (6) lobsters and starfish feed on the remains. Decomposers such as (7) bacteria and worms break down the last bits, which become part of the sand or mix with the water. Kelp absorbs these (8) nutrients directly from the water in addition to the energy that they receive from the sun. Then the whole cycle begins again.

Humans and Kelp Forests

People depend on kelp forests for many reasons. Humans use a chemical found in kelp, called algin, in hundreds of products such as latex rubber, ink, toothpaste, ice cream, and soup.

Kelp forests also provide rich fishing grounds that supply people with seafood such as lobsters, abalone, and sea urchins. Some methods of fishing can be destructive to kelp forest animals, though.

Global warming may influence kelp forests as well. Kelp forests can die when the water becomes warmer than 72°F (20°C). People may be able to help decrease global warming when they drive cars less, use cleaner energy sources such as wind and solar power, and plant more trees.

Kelp forests are rich fishing grounds, but some methods of fishing have harmed this important habitat.

Today, some people realize that kelp forests are an important habitat worth protecting. They have set aside protected areas such as the Monterey Bay National Marine Sanctuary in California. Fishing is not allowed there, and scientists can study kelp forest creatures in their natural environment. These areas should help ensure that kelp forests and their inhabitants will survive for many years to come.

The Marine Life Sanctuary in Pacific Grove, California, and other protected areas ensure the survival of kelp forests and the animals that make them their home.

A Kelp Forest's Food Web

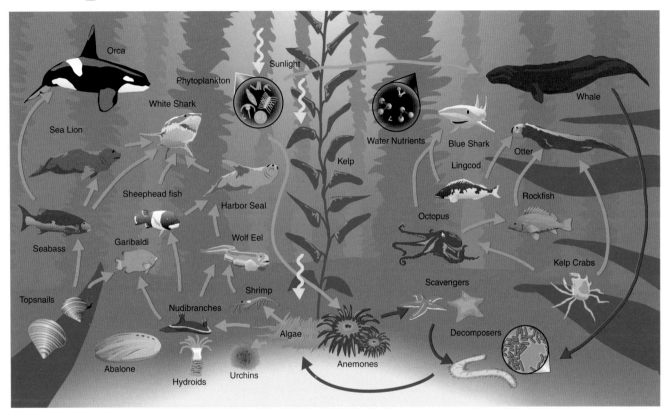

A food web shows how creatures in a habitat depend on one another to survive. The arrows in this drawing show the flow of energy from one creature to another. Yellow arrows: plants nourished by the sun; Green arrows: animals that eat green plants; Orange arrows: predators; Red arrows: scavengers and decomposers. Whatever is left becomes part of the water and is taken up by plants as part of their nourishment. The cycle repeats.

Glossary

Adaptation A change in the behavior or characteristics of a plant or animal that increases its chances of survival in a particular habitat

Algae Simple plants that do not produce roots or flowers; seaweeds are algae.

Camouflage A coloration or shape that allows a plant or animal to be hidden against its background

Canopy The top layer of the kelp forest, which is made up of the fronds floating on the surface

Decomposers Animals such as worms and bacteria that eat dead tissue and return nutrients to the water

Fronds The long, rubbery stalks that make up the kelp plant

Habitat The area in which a plant or animal naturally lives. A habitat provides living organisms with everything they need to survive—food, water, and shelter.

Holdfast The rootlike structure stuck to the reef that keeps the kelp plant from drifting away

Predators Animals such as sharks that hunt other animals for their food

Prey An animal killed and eaten by another animal

Reef Any surface on the ocean's bottom. A reef can be made of sand, coral, rock, and other materials.

Scavengers Animals such as starfish that feed on animals that are already dead.

Understory The middle layer of the kelp forest, which is made up of smaller kelp species such as winged and bull kelp

For More Information

Books

Davis, Chuck. *California Reefs*. San Francisco: Chronicle Books, 1991.

Hall, Howard. *The Kelp Forest*. San Luis Obispo, CA: Blake, 1999.

McLeish, Ewan. *Habitats: Oceans and Seas*. Austin, TX: Steck-Vaughn, 1997.

Web Sites

California Kelp Forests
www.jellieszone.com/kelpforest.htm *Monterey Bay Aquarium, Kelp Forest Exhibit*
www.mbayaq.org

Index